INTERVAL

Poems Based on Bach's *"Goldberg Variations"*

Alice B. Fogel

schaffner
press

SCHAFFNER PRESS

TUCSON, ARIZONA

Also By Alice Fogel

Poems

Be That Empty
I Love this Dark World
Elemental

Non-Fiction

*Strange Terrain: A Poetry Handbook for
the Reluctant Reader*

First Printing
Printed in the United States

Cover Photo: "Source" Courtesy of Lisa Robinson, granted by permission, all rights reserved.

Cover and interior design: James Kiehle

ISBN: 978-1-936182-72-5
E-Pub: 978-1-936182-74-9
Mobipocket/Kindle: 978-1-936182-73-2
Adobe: 978-1-936182-75-6

Schaffner Press, Tucson, AZ

Library of Congress Cataloging-in-Publication Data

Fogel, Alice (Alice B.)
[Poems. Selections]
Interval : poems based on Bach's "Goldberg Variations" / Alice B. Fogel. -- First edition.
     pages ; cm
  ISBN 978-1-936182-72-5 (softcover) -- ISBN 978-1-936182-73-2 (mobi-pocket) -- ISBN 978-1-936182-74-9 (epub)
  I. Title.
  PS3556.O277A6 2015
  811'.54--dc23
                          2014040879

Contents

The making of INTERVAL:
Poems Based upon Bach's *Goldberg Variations*

It is hard to grasp, least of all by any mental logic, how the mathematical manipulation of sound into a structure of combined and ordered pitches can break one's heart. What makes a certain interval between notes, a certain pace or tempo, a subtle inversion after repetition, rip open the range of human emotion? Easier to explain particle physics, or the evolution of romantic love—or the intervals we're allotted for our lives.

This project set out to explore not so much why music moves us as how it embodies the incorporeal. Perhaps we are like music in that we too amount to more than a particular, if fortuitous, arrangement of concrete matter. I wanted this series of poems to explore the theme of embodiment and spirit that music represents, while using musical forms as the poems' given structure. Music, a traceable construct on paper, rises off the page, passes through the senses, and leaves a lingering physical and spiritual ache beyond definition and form; this project was born from the urge to make a poetry that might do the same.

The more one learns about Johann Sebastian Bach, a religious man and a rigorous practitioner—and inventor—of musical forms, the more awed one becomes. I might go so far as to say there is no one who has surpassed him, but I am only an amateur musicologist, and I may just be hopelessly infatuated. For my purposes in creating a poetry of musical form both traditional and individually created, Bach's *Goldberg Variations* (*GV*) became my focus and my obsession. They include passages playful, tragic, stirring, meditative, wild, impassioned, hypnotic. As harpsichordist Kenneth Gilbert puts it, "the notes provide an astounding range of musical texture, thought, and feeling," and all this above a basic "obsessive and pulsating" ground.

My background training in and long and early exposure to classical music, along with some research supported by a National Endowment for the Arts Fellowship, helped me in studying the *GV* enough to gain a basic understanding of what Bach has done. Because *Interval* is based, in form and perceived content, on these pieces, this preface will attempt to briefly outline my understanding of how their entire system works.

As a whole, the *GV* constitute an elaborate superstructure, a gigantic chaconne, or dance, based on the ground bass in the left hand of the Aria, or opening piece. The entire Aria is repeated at the end, and between these two presentations are 30 variations, making 32 parts in all. Symmetrically, each variation itself consists of 32 measures, divided into two parts of 16 measures each. While the key remains consistent throughout as either G major or minor (which represents, for me and perhaps Bach, both "God," or, in German, "Gutt"— ineffable spirit—and the "Ground"—the physical root of the music), other aspects vary, such as time signatures and musical styles, which in themselves configure nearly the entire spectrum of dance or other musical forms in Europe in Bach's time.

The 30 variations are subtly halved into two groups of 15 (and if we consider the outside Arias framing them, the groups would each be, of course, 16), with the 15th variation ending in a kind of question and the 16th opening the second half with a bit of a bang (though not as forceful as that of the first) and taking the form of an overture.

The 30 pieces are also segmented into 10 groups of three. Every third variation is a canon, with overlapping, round-like voices imitating themes, and with these repetitions beginning at a different interval for each one. In other words, the first canon begins its counterpoint on the first or same note as the theme, canon #2 on the note a step above, or second, canon #3 on the third note, and so on, through nine canons, the final variation being an exception, a more colloquial or personal, melodic "quodlibet."

These triplet segments have been described as piers or pylons holding up a complex bridge. In addition to the last of each group of three being a canon, the second variation of each triad is often a toccata, and these are considered brief diversions from the more structured pieces surrounding them.

To mimic the musical structures of the *GV*, each poem in "Interval" is made up of two 16-line sections. In addition to formal considerations, the verbal variations reflect their corresponding musical variations in both direct and subtle ways, however subjectively interpreted, such as rhythm, temperament, tone of voice, mood, or phrasing. The liminal states of the poetic variations attempt to echo the link between music's concrete, mathematical elements and its abstract effects. Sensations of time expanding and contracting, the movements of overlapping and crossing over, and an expression of other dualities, are further themes whose phrases echo, repeat, and alter throughout.

Throughout the variations, Bach has created a baroque network of multiple voices which, in the poems, I tried to mimic in the following ways. First, counterpoint (harmony, the layering of pitches) is a kind of vertical texture, unlike simple melody (comparable to narrative line), which is horizontal. The layering of word sounds over syntax and sense creates the same vertical texture effect in a poem. Next, with the exception of the centerpieces of each triad, described above, every poem has a particular speaker, identified in the title—an "I" (or "we"), addressing an implied or stated "you," and at times referring to a third party or parties ("them"). As influenced by the range of musical forms or voices Bach employed, these personae represent a range of actual, though fictional, living entities of differing ages, genders, species, time periods, and life circumstances, often fleeting.

Exploring self and being, the identified voices each speak either about or from a threshold state—a brief or lingering interval between more recognized or stable aspects of life or death. By contrast, the second variations of each group of three represent a state of being, often with no "I" at all, or else with a dis- or un-embodied or otherwise unformed identity. These interlude poems' titles appear in italics.

Finally, the poems in *Interval* are not meant in any way to be librettos or lyrics or any other sort of accompaniment. Bach himself was known to indulge in "translating" or reinterpreting other musicians' work, and these poems came about through that kind of borrowing. For their form and ideas and inspiration, I am grateful to Bach's *Goldberg Variations*.

Interval

Aria

All phases have beauty. Or in shaping time
was Bach lost to all but the count, not consonance?

One in the other, carriage and contained,
body and spirit, hitched, indivisible:

From the ground up with fractal scaffolding
he built his arc, this liquid bridge for the daily

practice of sameness, sequence, awaking
change, the brief, the sustained—and the enduring

whole bears as one all notes, as one word might
all said or sung. Where does it come from, the material

of the beautiful? And how aligned or skewed
toward discord, how reasoned with ardor and risk,

how little or much design or dumbfound—
how can we know? Grave, heavenly,

like the illumined face of a god rubbed from stone,
these breaths so wholly numbered and numinous . . .

A mere miracle of physics? Mathematics' holy writ?
Most musical web of ordered intervals framed

by symmetry, division, multiples—most melancholy
joy: Ten parallel horizons zenithed

toward always, thirty-two limiting longitudes:
A language, a form, a key. God, Johann: When in thrall

a pianist's hands arch intimate
to make the passage—to touch

your immortal body—it is as if the finite, bound,
has unwound when your *now* becomes now anew,

now mine. As if thresholds allowed recrossing: Forever
to be content, a soul at home, with a life like art

more puzzle than plan, more flight than counterweight,
the perfect grid of abiding piers upon which you

superimpose the moving force
of brilliant ephemera . . .

Variation 1: Yhwh

Explode from the cauldron dark,
that's what I'd do for them: That in mind into self

and other I divided. In and in I overlapped in density
and where I was gravid I breathed their breaths.

With my body like a brine spiraling I stirred
the silence till it echoed apart from me, and where I

was deafened I hummed their frequencies.
From a floating ground I fired rounds of clouds

flaming and where they burned I brewed the rutilated
light till it refracted in the wells between comets rocketing.

In and in through the ancient rooms I fell and where
there were thresholds I left them canyons gorgeous

and aggrieved. Flung wide, electrified, I striated skies
with ellipsis, color, collapse, shot suns past

eclipse, blew the air for sound to sound
from touch, touched them till they cried in ecstacy:

Out and out and through the skin my sweat
ran and poured into hollows so where I emptied

they filled and though I encompassed
they merely contained. Into the molten cavity I

dropped a stone, I lit the furnace, stretched a hide.
I wielded the ragged white-veined ice and birthed

spinning galaxies in atoms, vital alluvium, the eternal
quest for me. I remembered and made them

forget. I raged and sweetened them. Formless then
I dimensioned space, delineated them. I swallowed

my own throat to feed them hungers delicious.
Where I could not pass I corridored their heavens.

Where I felt nothing I caused them passion and urge.
I watch them and they are blind to me.

I lie awake, and they dream.
I cry out to them, and they die.

Variation 2: Interval

If in the temporal world
of the measure

of plenitude that spans
the vast interstice

hanging in the balance
between the invocation

and the prayer—O
holiest interval—there

were no mercy and God
the invention said yes

I'm here you rang
why tarry Say

yes yes I am ready
Death is for being

done
with finitude:

If in the temporal plenitude
the measured world hung

in that vast spin If in the world
of interstice measured in balanced spans

If in the hung invocation—O Lord—
/—O World!—the prayer were no mercy

If God tarried in if If in the unmeasurable interval
the holy plenitude of yes a merciful intervention

If God rang in the balance
between here and the holy

why why invoke the vast tally if
between ready and death God said yes

you prayerful span of being
I am done I am death

for finitude why say
if why is.

Variation 3: Snapping turtle

Borne forward by extended increments.
        Crawling waterward from this weed wilted shore.

Like small furred voles skittering inward, taking little
        grounded, mirrored steps: Like this, intervals of ice

ridge and rime the pond rim. By night. As if
        by dreaming ice might cast its million limbs

over that surface above. Its frozen tincture
        outfolding farther, farther unfurling across. By dawn:

The moonspread scales then a foregone conclusion.
        Constructed, transmutable truth: All day ice

shrinking from the light, reconsidering.
        And still, in leaving, leaving its lingering

doubt, pale shadow of wingspan edgebound.
        Near. Then again in dark the cold falling, fallen

to glow on the meniscus, ice groping forward with more
        sliding white. Ice: Its own logic, growing:

Its horizontal precipice. Its glass
      carapace. Night's cold and hoary

frost. Vaster still till all its heirs' outstretched
      tips interslip, imprint with their ferny whorls

an entire span between lands.
      To travel that unthinkably far! And then, having reached

to cry out *more room!*—crack
      like a shell, heave between its crushing shores.

But which pressing which? And what boundary
      divides water from ice, what self

solidifies against self, which is water—host or
      whore? Ice now in spring dissolving, dissolute

reversal by increments retreating. Not I,
      alive, here mudnudged under eaves, forming

my young egg by egg, mother's lasting bequest.
      To nest once in heat. To hatch and be born.

Variation 4: Child

When I asked them at breakfast I said
when will I get the shots? and what shots?

Mama said, and how could she forget
that dog, the way the eagle circled over me,

I thought at first it would hurt me but it had lifting
me in the sky on its mind, rescue

from the dog who was pale and foamed
like the river sometimes does and she

scared the eagle away. So amazed I said
don't you remember the bite?

and she smiled and it was true
it had healed overnight. Behind Mama's door

I hid myself where only her long mirror is allowed
to see me cry and him the size a person ought to be.

Just one making two, crayon-crayons
touching like a kiss we drew together

one tree between, and I liked the way his hand
was my hand too. The tree grew out of a rock

the way I saw them down by the river
and I said I will hurry up and waste no time

and he said I will slow down like a tree
that loves a rock so well it will grow from it

and I laughed because they don't
know, because when I asked where

will you go when you die and who
will love me then she said a little thing

like dying is not enough
to kill my love for you but tomorrow

I will have to ask again because look
what happened with the eagle and the dog

that she forgot today. I am the only one
around here who knows.

Variation 5: Spinning

spinning   I thought I might not yet infuse
        myself   not yet breathe my life   into a living thing

I would not embody   I breathed   was breath
gathered in and unspooled out   rhythm   lung   folding

        fan   expanding and contracting in
in spin   I was dizzying

        the dust   scattering debris of meteors   splintering
memory oncoming I spilled   in and out infinities   looping

back and back through empty airless   corridors
        banks of starless dark

spun and lapped and webbed   I traveled far
        made no choice   fast   unfastened   spinning free

I was winds of unsung atmospheres   a legend of spinning
heavens   their planets   and the great   unbreathing spaces

        between   down to universes
down to spiral and parallel

spinning   I thought I'd play one planet in symmetry
        in spin   I breathed

was breath   was the whirled breaths of all the living   the being
as yet and not yet   the wheeled and flared   breath spinning

        and splitting   the eye inside unseeing and I
the spinning   the world   breath   living wind   I so close

        but still not   choosing   spinning   until
brushed by the rush of solids against   winds

until like a lintel   I was the place between them   above
        the surface where cliffs crest hard broken

through crust   risen and bound   back down
        where water and wetlands slide and tie

the moon to mountainsides   where earth's skin meets
the smoothing   the sculpting   resistant winds

        of all the infinite rest   still   I was this   the spinning
thin   membrane of distance between them

Variation 6: Snake

Have use of edges.
Alongside field—crosshatch trees

to their meadow pedestal.
Way is seam

here beneath eaves where when further
forest rises and effaces sun

camouflaging silver bleed
congeals. Smaller than rivers

go sleek like rivers and like
rivers slip unseen

below earthly surface things—
pour with invisible volition

between storm-tamped
weeds—slip clear

through stone to lick
fresh linings of eggs.

Chromatic curvature—scale
horizon's arc littered with all

closest slightest movements
of toad and vole—small

measures of hungry sight.
More beautiful than wind more

grounded than birds
more clever and calm

than time what more
need for body than this:

To crush sloughed leaves
with slim sounds no louder in heaven

than none—migrate
through tunnel skin meant to briefly

burrow in—emerge
clean removed and hunt whole again.

Variation 7: Girl

I never told you because you'd make this big fuss
and do some fucking ritualistic

hang-your-panties-from-the-weeping-
cherry-tree-in-the-yard sort of thing—/—oh

you never told me it would be like something hot liquifying
my thighs, like a hot seabed dragging its craggy stones

down my back. / In fact you never mentioned this: /
intrusion from within. /—Just because your mother wouldn't

talk about it and her mother slapped her face
and who knows what all the mothers did before that,

cover them with earth and wine, chant hymns to the goddess.
If I ever have a daughter here's all I'm going to do:

say, That's nice honey, or You go girl, or whatever
is hip when she's 13 and let her pierce anything she wants.

/ Or the stain like a tattooed rose on my clothes.
Can I please stay home?

/ I'm fine. / Well maybe unsteady on my feet
as if just coming to shore. Rocking, rocking. Mutiny.

Strange lands. I spiral that island, spinning, aswim.
/ Yeah I know I can get pregnant now, but I'm not

planning to just yet. Don't worry, Mom,
I think I can give you till my junior year at least.

Why do you need to know that?—I threw them away.
I gave them to my boyfriend, I'm making a pillow.

Maybe I burned them—with incense
and smudge sticks and a ring of virgin girls. /

You can put your hand over my forehead /
but stop talking. I already know what to do. /

Cross the moat to the haunted house, that ancient castle
of rooms inside rooms that just opened one more door.

Sure / whatever / we'll plant flowers where I buried
the panties. / Fucking flowers, Mom. / *Maybe they'll even grow.*

Variation 8: Request

It is the watershed of blood that I want, and all
other salty smooth liquids: Semen, vaginal waters

elastic and streaked, sweat in its miniscule pearled
drops or as streams, saliva, urine, tears. Blood

will sustain, shape and color me, contain
itself in a skin to stay within or seep beyond.

Skin is what I need, a paper to inscribe and swirl
my design upon. Skin to press to the ground,

skin to press into skin or soft tissue, slender cells
that expand and fill within as organ, or as muscle.

It is muscle that I want, fists of firm fluidity
thriving inside, curving to move the movable.

Uterus. Tongue. Heart. Penis muscling its skin
upward with blood. Long veins to stretch and harden

through muscle into tendon, ligament:
God, for the lineaments of a life:

The blessed limit to where I can go, who to be, body
formed finally and only of luck

and called biology. All of a piece: Blood's
same substance for its arteries, same material for its skin,

muscle, tendon, pain and range, and a name solid as bone:
All the matter that matters, all the life that lives.

Oh I must have the bones, that plain rigidity.
Give me flute and hammer, socket, ball

and skull. To stand up on my own confined
soles, open only so wide my only two human

blooded, breakable arms! That I might come entering
the seed of a new inkling, the knowing that *I am*,

the beginning and the end, and reach
the air with bones and blood and skin crying aloud because

it is breath, breath, breath that I want, and my own
hollows to heave it through.

Variation 9: Potter

Wheel of becoming, wheel of twin firmaments, I work you round
   wheel of becoming, wheel of twin   seasons, earth cupped

firmaments, I work you round   in my rough hands, slip water
   seasons, earth cupped   over the island

in my rough hands, slip water   of clay on the heavenmost
   over the island   circle, warm to the fire

of clay on the heavenmost   of friction turning under my feet
   circle, warm to the fire   its body upraised with breath

of friction turning under my feet   I pull past each shape
   its body upraised with breath   my own surface in flux over the bending

I pull past each shape   bones within, the clay changing
   my own surface in flux over the bending   like air exhaled by the moment

bones within, the clay changing   and my fingertips lose their swirling
   like air exhaled by the moment   lines that imprint me as unique

and my fingertips lose their swirling   fill with the swelling red medium
   lines that imprint me as unique   predicting my future

fill with the swelling red medium   absence
   predicting my future   at the same time

absence   the clay takes my identity
   at the same time   stealing the infinitesimal designs

the clay takes my identity   of my skin for its own smooth side
   stealing the infinitesimal designs   another and another shape it isn't

of my skin for its own smooth side   taking its place in, in the spinning nape
   another and another shape it isn't   of its risen working, its sliding

taking its place in, in the spinning nape   ride between opposing fissions
   of its risen working, its sliding   of my fingertips soon one "I" fixed

ride between opposing fissions   in time, after all the spun
   of my fingertips soon one "I" fixed   worlds of I's

in time, after all the spun   but
   worlds of I's   not yet

but   not yet
   not yet, not yet.

Variation 10: Moths

Long once, hung from oaks, dangled rungs of boneless
flesh webbed in open nets among branches, the green

edgy leaves rotten limp. Fantastic scourge of furred
black columns balanced from lanky cords spit

from our own dumbstruck mouths. O the life in the trees,
our weighted fringe slung over roofs and streets, that rapt

business of crawling in the sun, the great solidity.
Now our dank houses tight wound all down our sides—

all sides that we are—and what did we do to deserve this wrap
inside time out outside of time, hidden, as if repentant

and intent upon resurrection? Our only actuality anticipation,
so becoming to itself. What do you take us for?

All right, it's true, we're lying here stupid, duped.
So that after this, all at once one fine night, shaken,

we can come to as little moths, cute
and foolish as flakes of summer snow and all for what—

we ask you. One slanting flurry of florid white wing
spilling, one feeble pulse of flight against the wrist

of one midnight: at dawn dismissed
to wisp and stillness, royal carpets of broken

wing flipped and swept across the expanse
and left to highlight every crack already veined

on roadways. Should we look forward to a flick
of life first as circle and cloud amassed

at streetlamps and then dropped, nearly done for,
a sweep of creeping outline, a brief and pallid grout

between the permanent stones? O we
once the sinewed, we the firm, we the chewing length

of leaf and stem squirm and warm, banned
to those slight cursive runes scrawled into crevices

and coiled along ditches like over-elongated reminiscences,
mere wan traces, of our darker former selves.

Variation 11: Reflection

Out in the center, canoe and you no cause
 for interruption (only

  wingless here while hovering)
   deep into water's overlaps the moon's

    fractures fold and flow, flow and fold and fracture.
    Look down long enough, out here on the lake

  afloat, surrounded by (and on) the dark lap
 lapping, the long wet folded fan moon, stippled

 length of twine moon, broken linked moon
  hanging its white chains down

   (as if down)
    into depths only visible

    horizontally, and all that dripped thick liquid
  ellipsis seems its own true form. Pierced

  by lunar rays, by turns
 the ponderous bass diminish and flash

bleeding upward from beneath
into the gleam and reach

of lit glissando. Opaque, steady
above all, the cool sky scoops

all that soaked, unskeined light up
into one flat coin, one disk like a wrist-

flicked stone you once skimmed like this
from shore that left no trail

of white. Fixed, dry, nearly
untouched, still that full moon pulled down

here across the waving layers
of slick lake slapping and

licking the gunwales skips downward, through
and through, illuminating water's

(buried and drowned)
ground by ruse.

Variation 12: Happy Prince* statue's bird

You, bejewelled as the pharoahs,
could have emptied the purse of winds

scented with snow and asked for nothing more.
But *take my ruby,* you wished, *to the seamstress,*

my emeralds to the match girl crying in the rain.
How did you know—with only stones to show

street lamps' reflection on your face— to feed
the hungry each one crust? Feet of clay, you

didn't need eyes, gem or otherwise. Nor ears
to hear the ceaseless weeping from gutter

to garrett, nor voice to persuade me to give
what wasn't mine to take. *Let me fly to Egypt*

tomorrow, I'd hum, *though I grow numb*
with cold today. As if possessed, against

my will, I kept stripping between the blades
of my beak all the gold that clothed you.

I sowed it in the streets where the poor cherished
and traded it for bread and ale and time

already running out. Already winter.
Too late for migration. Too late even for you

who could not go on and on giving because,
foolish Prince, suffering is by far a greater cache

than gold. Beloved, you don't need a body
to feel the yearning of a soul. While the living's palm

still like a tomb lies bare, all that giving lost
in the streets' turns and fares, both of us once gilded

break, flung down from the pedestal, bereft.
Too late to warm me, your body burnt,

your heart beside me scarab-bright and shining
in the dust. Too late for the Nile, your ashes flying

over the city like swallows
leaving for the south.

* The "Happy Prince" is a statue in Oscar Wilde's story of the same name.

Variation 13: Artist

Later, when mud sops upward, sodden with gone or transformed snow,
and I am left to trace in black and white from memory

more than ground and sky, this is what I will most miss: that other
kind of tree that though unfallen curved in crosshatch toward me,

that concatenous, suspended, horizontal tree:
The one that needed snow as page, as mirror, door. Those trees

in snow dimension dip deep into downward folds, bend up the other slope—
strips beribboning snow in palettes of white and gray, almost blue,

rippling as if in wind. Like paths of water
snow's trees flow and flex and in slow spin turn daily as one waving

to the sweep of sun. From the edge of growth where slender trunks darkly
ache toward sky, snow trees—a second, perpendicular, forest—

lie down to rest. I will miss how, in hollows carved by the flux
of snow-buried land, snow trees

were the scuffed and open fingers of the limb cupped from vertical trunks
outward and happy to be earthbound.

They reach across distances icy and untrammeled.
Too warm this afternoon. For how much longer now

can snow be another place, neither earth nor air,
that takes the shadow of a high tree and draws it down in its own

negative light? Draw everything—
the density of trees, sprawled weeds, waves of shadow and shade—

everything else but the snow and still the snow is there. Snow
here, and here, all in between things, irrefutable existence, and a vision

like what the dying might see in the mind's new eye, shaped
by oncoming memory, or outlined by the failure

of a heart. How many more days
across the shore of this shining field will real trees reach their snow

trunks down, go impossible lengths, into the illusory depth
fathomless in these few feet of snow? I want to plunge my hands

down to grasp them, scrub their gathered skins
hard into my palms, but I know what I will hold: Only cold.

Variation 14: Here after

After what will happen has happened and is done:
                    Begin.

        Here in the infinity of aftermath
                    in the dying echo of the echo

    died down, in the dark patch after
                    the last light flash.

        In the pain of knowledge
after the knowledge of pain: In everything.

Every subject rimed with the undeniable
            what happened   now however much

                    denied. No place beyond
its blistered realm, no

                    time outside its frame.
Every word uttered wrung from it.

        Every gesture touched with it, every
expression visibly limned with its brine.

In the quickened heart of its doneness
               in the radius of its eternal dissolve.

        Never the dispelled ever the dispelling.
Regardless of giving up forever the given.

                        Irrelevant to forgetting.
Henceforth, no or

               yes, the vast, vast after.
                        Inescapable atmospheric

overpopulated prehistoric continent of afterness.
        Useless regret for, no return to, untenable

        grieving over, unattainable relief from
               the irretrievable unrelivable *before*.

Happened happened happened. But after, after—!
Begin. In the life hereafter, in the long obsessive

        moment after the moment after after after
what would happen did happen and is done.

Variation 15: Woman at the dam

I like to think my soles with sloshing footsteps pressed
a few drops more from the source, that spring underground

where the brook slipped free. Like an acolyte
I followed its liquid tongue,

the path it was carving still down the long hillside.
Then how many others like me, over time, have stepped out

of these same trees deep in woods and into
this surprise of lake cradled as if in eternity, and I

never more mortal? Sudden slow lake strapped in
by stick walls mudded with earth and roots, brush and living

weeds, so that I have to—every *I* has to—
look up to the water's surface as I stand beside its belly.

How many years' repeated rhythms of beavers' lives transforms
one damp bottomland into a mimicry of sea? How many generations'

turns at the wheel? How long ago the breeze bending to a new tune
on the elevated shore above an altered floor?

I lean my body today against the earthbound wall, lend my arms
as branches, bend into the cold trickle seeping down

the dam, imagine I'm holding all this in, infinitesimal
wet piece of forever, fluid force in the shape of a stream

including me: Clear water runs its course through my jeans, washes
my feet, jaunts on from its forgotten pond, into wetlands

where deer graze and coyotes stalk and capture them, on back
into denser woods, scrawling its signature under an illiterate sky.

No beavers here today where every body of water spans its finite time
and every soul is a guest. No deer, no one at all but I. And

phantom wind, eerie waves in a fiction, an inland imitation
of ocean ebb and flow. No far horizon in this bowl of pond and trees.

No moon pull, nor enough sun to cast my shadow onto you,
dear weird earth, lifted ground—for are you more certain or unmoved

over time than I, as laughable and accidental here
in sodden shoes as you?

Variation 16: Actor

So. Call me obtuse, it isn't what you think. My angle
on method? It's not some avoidance tactic softshoe

get-me-out-of-*me* shuffle, ta-ta
I'm off to transcend. No, it's a hallelujah

chorus raising the rafters in the theatre
of souls that passes as my skull. Wait up, MacDuff,

attention must be paid. *That's* why I do it—to let each
make a scene center-stage, because *personality*,

you know, is death-defying, that's right, it's all an act
in the wings, and I am as many I's as Zeus

gave Argus and honey, I strut them
like a peacock, in top form. Call me a dodo, I am not

extinct when like a bird I fly the coop of earthly bounds,
equity transmigration, toasting a born again role.

I take a fresh soul home with each new script,
and honey, I *can* go home again.

And again and again. What you see
is not who I *am*: In my one

singular sensational shape I don and slough a slew
of disparate selves. Think it's distraction I'm after, anything but

humble little me? Don't you just wish
you could live once in this be-costumed bod, and die

night after night, and die, and die, and *die*, and still—wonders—*be*
this attractive? Call me vain. Shameless. I'm saving face-

lifts by means of masks. An I for an I? Sleight of hand?
Out of body experience? Honey, it's all here in my vita.

Call me a condiment, in solid standing,
fluid when handled and poured. Over-

soul, when called I come: It's sexy but not
sexual, lovely but hardly love, escapade, yes,

but never escape. All entrancing and never having
to bow out. So call me any time. Any one.

Variation 17: Like waking

Will death be like this? Like waking
from a long dream

still held—grounded—
in the body disremembered? Spinning

ceiling, close call? Foolish beating
heart? Those trembling

aftershocks of some electric message
where bone met motion,

clamoring in ligaments,
that lingering tremolo singing in the ears

like doubt, maybe
the echo of some unrecognized

once-familiar name. Estranged touch
of wind over skin,

on damp arms the hair
not yet laid down . . .

Breath's sour fluctuations
not quite tamed. Cheeks' flush

loosening, a displaced temperature
sensed, unseasonal. Flash of light

burning against walls, image after image,
an eye, a frame, missing there.

Where, searching, searchless, you can't point to
or put a finger on, nevertheless an urge

surging in raised fingers. A circle
discontinuous, once rounded out by mouth.

Throbbing inside the brow,
no accessible thought. Specifically

no memory arising from
follicles still tingling, the dulling skull heedless,

singed with salty pores.
What if it's like this, only without the body?

Variation 18: Baker

Always daily in darkness deeper
than the former lit room of my dreams

I rise to predawn. By daybreak already
the bread side by side like cobblestones

baking in the great black womb,
its spirit scent ascending:

that sweetness that bitterness
absorbs and then sets free. Always already

the wheat in the field, hunger, rain.
The stalks in the bleeding

hand, grain
in the mill, chaff on the ground.

Grain ground until
all air's banished, all spaces fill

with the lighter heavier
powder of flour:

Then once more in the solid
dough, pushing, breath-infused, inspired,

the yeast singing from the heart
always already wine-alive,

releasing, like some tiny muse being
compressed, so the more I press, the more

it rises up—soprano prayer
returning to God and soon to be

folded into well-oiled forms. And by day
always already I have swallowed

steaming the broken
wholeness of fresh-grown loaves,

the aboriginal substance a language selved
warm in my throat, another

expanded breast's intake of air
firmed in the famished flesh.

Variation 19: Fish

Bathed is the world   lucid   made of fluid
and motion motion and fluid translucence.

Close.   Cool and fluttering
and full. This is   suspension and fins

sliding   through weeds and slices
of light culled down.

Air mote filtering   filigree   water mote
afloat. Wet sameness light

along all sides. This   the world
a surrounding. Dull gray soundings

off grounded reefs   of rocks and roots
of islands. Soothing

color blends   in bellies' scales
that descend decrescendo   in the deep

blues of home. Between   bottom silt
and quaver   of meniscus: the silence:

All the world spread wide: water
water water.   Water turning

foodwater   sleepwater.
Water push and pull. Wait.

Dash. Waterhold. This is the wash
pulse place   world and time   wet.

Not
that place of gasp and

nothing   vastness   the dementia
of waterless where I was lifted

on a line extended   from a point
beyond   blinding and sharp

and whirring   and not
the grasp

that flung me
back from that dry death.

Variation 20: Duration

In the law of distances never crossed
      that place destination's adamant

      along the azimuth gazed upon the greatest
degree of longing either will

cleave the avenue of approach or longer prevent
arrival: Such is your spiritual virga.

      In the field the grass blade's tip
waves its small hand of heat and snow

falling evaporates beyond the reach of what it meant
to kiss. Long ago when you lay once abed

      your parents' voices grazed you
but not the sense of their sounds: Why

then that was comforting when
across time from them now you crave their word.

      Do you think the lilies long to bloom
above the trees above earth's atmosphere in heavens?

Strain to bridge from buried root sheer
to suffocating sky the vertigal leaps to enlightenment?

Their failure their limited range: Not theirs. For
          how high is high enough?—to reach what?

How long is long enough to stem
the inevitable to live to say what find what do

what what else before—what? The touching
gesture between birth and burning the two beams

that interlock the crossed quadrants is the key: We
of this earth might be God's interverse:

          All spirit
has of the sensate: We the children the lilies

the grass: Longing longing longing:
For more. Or to endure. In death as in life. To swear

to take this body to love honor and obey it take it
          as death does its part.

Variation 21: Dying man

Like walking, though walking's done: / Some iambic, twofold step the body takes:

An unbalancing balancing. Like living in two / days dawned between the same

two nights—in one / day dying, in the other quickening to life.

One where you still walk—your day— / the other dayless bright. It takes

two days to die like this, takes one / foot grounded, one hovering—day in

and day out alternating. In: Out: It's / like breathing: Oh—world still here! World

gone again. Know its disappearance only / by its return—or mine. Love with you

was like that too—another day's welcome / little daily death:

Only to be you—be in you, out of self—you / then me again. Out: Don't miss you now,

love, or me. Lifted: Forget. / Watch light spread.

A tidepool flashing with faces / from the other days. Try to remember

to tell you. Day in: Know you / would like to know. Out a lake of relations, all

expecting me. In—out—an ocean on the day / you call in today, a homeless day out

in light of horizonless space. Out. Day / in. Still there—you and you—and you—

awaiting me on either side. / So many crossings before the given

day. In. Can still feel you / —out—there but ah—I am walking here—

Variation 22: Equivocator

Say that love *is* a love that cannot die.
So that if it does it is not a matter neither

created nor destroyed and isn't love.
Or was it? So that to have loved and lost

is never to have loved at all: Can love
never die with impunity? Is suicide

love's only way out? Say love is molecular,
pheromones, phoneme, idea: Can't it have two

or more sides? What if the loved object dies
and the love is without object, then what

is the object of love? Or if the object lives—
I know, I know, I know but let's just say—

but the love takes another subject to love.
Can love not translate, multiply, commute?

Can love never be pluperfect nor plural,
would you have it be censored, suppressed?

Say love *was* a love that died.
Say love never loved, did what it pleased,

made its own choices, got a cat. Or that
a love unloved was nevertheless itself

a love, and could. If it wanted.
Say love is a love defined by love itself,

loves itself, knows nothing
but itself, is always one

and the same: Is love a mirror, a point,
spiral, sphere, a line? What? So say love

could wait for us to die
to die. Or could wait forever to love

its true love, who's waiting, so that in waiting
to love it's still a love, although

true, unloved, and so perhaps is dead,
unless that isn't love.

Variation 23: Teatime

Watch that pot: held at first
      at bay, embarking: wait

   for the heat like mirage
to form small continents

     of air bursting into boiling's
becoming: secret celebration at striking

    out for the territories, all this
stormy steaming fuss and ruckus

     raised high to heaven the noise
of a joy released as if resistance

    all war whoop and turning
all passage and canal: coolness dispelled

    misgiving giving in, giving
way like scree on cliffsides

    sliding into oceans' deeper
pockets of stone: a kind of migration:

this bridge made by striding
mad meridians island after risen

island across a far horizon to the heaven
of *now*: wait: and watch:

how like the soul, this liquid, to love
to fight the forces

of change and then surrender
to currents and sail

without ephemerides finally wild
through confusions—to spring unwound

at last the great escapement: this loud
beating at the hull a strafing, a stepping

stone between poured fluid simply still
and the streaming roll and hum

and wave of water newly
ready for infusion.

Variation 24: Leatherman

Humming once in a walking daydream on the narrow wooded trail,
when unaware of where I was, was in fact not even there,

I entered the deep smell of animal, brown, sweated, dense.
Like a sudden memory in the body upon waking

or a realization too late come, it came to me only as I crossed
over the line of it. But different, this time, it lingered—

and I could go back: I turned back into the must,
breathed the life—still breathing—of what was left behind: a present

in the wake of what had passed. So close that I dwelled
in it and it clothed me:

the physical spirited through the trees,
an embodiment disembodied without death: that animal odor

whetted me as if with the forest's own rough tongue.
Charged, I stood in the woods, in the full

smell of a barn with neither livestock nor walls, of a thing
set free to prey:

I knew animal then. I became
animal in the beaten misshaped leather

of my clothes and shoes and some animal crouched or stretched
knew me: In a world of scents I knew my own self for once

was a missive meant to be received, taken from the flesh—
was itself a kind of flesh, a spirit bread arisen,

shed and left and soon perceived. Always sloughed afar,
and already in and of my newest, closest skin.

Alerted, my heart spun and sped in such a physical presence
of mind, such a clear and present sign. Then beast and I

must breathe the same language: I listened for it with the same
thirsty sense that gulped its word so fiercely

in the dark pit of my throat. And walk the same ground:
I saw the fresh tracks in the earth I pressed that spring

as I stepped forward again singing some unmeasured
long time later.

Variation 25: Freed slave

One thing for sure I like to do is climb right back into bed
after I fly out and remember then I got nobody's worrying to fly out for.

Then in my dress Miss Helen give me on account of her mama's blueberry
pie over the breastbone where I sewed a posie of strips cut from inside

the hem, I tend the garden, all mine. Okra and snap beans swing tight
in sheaths of green over rough silk beet leaves, onions in dirty brittle

petticoats below. All the same, the way they grow. Like folks' sweat
on their bodies and clothes, food, mud, dust, all the same, even now

when I got washing my living and my life. Early on I learned because how
I liked the water and how no matter the dingy gray or dark of the bar,

suds always come out white frothy as acacia blossoms in May.
I thought too it might wash me clean. Miz Clara's poplin tea-and-honey

stripes I got to scrub the back of most, and lay in sun face down,
cause how the front's so faded from her standing long hours at the south

window waiting. Could be I'm waiting, not meaning to, trying not
to remember what it was I used to worry back then. Expecting it

to show up uninvited at my door. On the washboard I gentle the calicos
from the two Misses Jones before dawn down the bakery

powdering their sleeves with ground wheat, growing plump as potatoes
on dough, only aprons to cover the fraying of their dresses' threads

at the bodice seams. Could be too late to learn to laugh like them.
Could be I'm most like Miz Charity's child keep trying to be born

and not be born, all the soap and soda and sun won't bleach out
the sheet stains that little white woman smuggles to me,

three times now in these two years I been here free. She not much more
than a girl herself, not like me. Someday they tell that child, like they told me,

You free now, but who do they mean me to be, who that *you* they say,
born and raised up not and now supposed to be? One thing

for sure I know is how brown the clear water grows with every press
and ring, that white lather soaked away invisible into cloth, all the dirt

let loose in the basin, unwanted. Evenings I pour it careful
on the roots of my okra, beets, my onions and snap beans.

Variation 26: Winter solstice

As if refracted in the least light—darkness's success
   and its successor—sixteen tangent dimensions aligned,

     their light fallen, paralleled, and raised
and just before we blinked we saw that where they crossed

     the darkest day of the year shone like a hard black stone
       at earth's core buried just before earth's surface closed:

So we stood at first in fear thinking it the end
   and for the first time believing in gods' departures,

     just before we saw the dark come to rest
and in that sole moment hovering

     blackbright in bittersweet hesitation between
       the pulling elements, between the leanings

of early against late or spring against fall, for once fully
   alive between heartbeat and unanticipated

     heartbeat, and hammocked in the rutilated paths
       of darkness's inversions, we felt

like the sea's hold just before its ebb's next flow,
the shore's design just before the tide reconfigures shore

or like the island just before its last ledge leaves
mainland's eroded side—ground slipping away

under first rain just before it opens to grow moist,
seed cradled just before it splits, the fat fruit's fermata

just before the touch that tips it from the vine—
like the body's silent O just before the taste of kiss,

the new mother's threshold just before the birth,
pain's mercy just before wounds hurt,

waking's shadow of doubt before sleep, memory's waver
just before remembrance, just before forgetting,

like the pendulum's linger just before—the involuntary urge
interrupted just—the step's still suspension—the halted

breath, rupture, edge, and also our own selves webbed,
abandoned and not yet taken by the time oncoming.

Variation 27: Awakener

In the recovery room, that wasteland
swelling around each separate safe

of anaesthesia, I witnessed the disfigured,
the only-partially human, the neither

dead nor alive: abandoned
fallacies of selves

desperate in borrowed beds.
Bough broken, in the bone-

naked light I saw instead their
demon spirits, gruesome, writhing

like Hell's own night-consumed souls.
Their emptied eyes bulged

from skulls, their formless shapes suspended
between shrouds of gray stained sheets,

the force of life like a witless bean
still jumping, spasmodic, inside.

From over distant thunder of ceiling fans
pushing the sickening air fell

the groans of the dispossessed:
They called *Help me, help*, cried *Mother*,

pleaded *Is anybody there?* I heard
their shocked and shameless moans as feeling

stomped back into organs and limbs
when the luscious numbness of the drugs

wore off. I wondered in my
strapped paralysis if one awful voice was mine.

Each part of my body snapped unwelcomed
back into time—cracked and pinned,

bruised and stitched—and I wanted nothing
but to return to the salvation

of oblivion from which I hurtled
unwillingly toward recovery.

Variation 28: Transplanted heart

Ooh we loved that bike. As good as sex, better sometimes,
not having to talk or think, not even of ourself. Bodiless, blasting

speed was the point, and everything moving was inside him
where I beat calm but charged, and outside, beyond,

our sitting body vibrating between both frictions and his riding
a meditation upon nothing. After the crash, I went on nodding

in some kind of nutty affirmative he refused. Like that science
experiment in seventh grade, when he carried the heart of an emptied

frog on a sodden paper towel all day through his classes, to see how long
it could live without its life: Sucking in its tiny side like a toy, liquid and firm

on desk after desk, it beat and beat, beating and waiting
in that perverse emancipation like an uprooted

seedling never headed for soil: Not that we would ever have thought
to put it that way. But then like that I beat too, though I could never

wake him, as if out of habit or in defiance, I ran, unstopped, for him and us,
even when decanted like some dark wine poured free from its broken jug:

See what I mean—it's *she* who loves the speed
of her own momentum and mind. If he'd ever had a chance

to know her, he would have liked her, not that we would have known her,
otherwise. Twice as old as he was and still young, now she's the one

I feed--so that I am a boy who never became a man,
and a woman who never was a girl. Ooh we love to swim,

to turn swimming into a flush of motion whose tides
are my own blood in her ears. It is one confused beauty his boy rhythms

pump into her woman limbs. Nights, she dreams me the ungrown
man herself, still strangers. When she begins to remember him, I forget

myself in the arc of her ecstacies, and wake him into her, pushing
always through her veins, inspire her to live again, as mine.

Didn't I twice beat time? Now when I flow into myself her him, heart
and soul wave and undertow, we relive

every dream that died in his crushed head, and dreaming
she calls out his name, the one we know by heart.

Variation 29: Boats

Boat after boat after boat after boat
hulls bottom up beside the hushed lake, cold

abandoned boats, scaled notes up and down
along the staff of shore. Boat after boat after boat

pulled up the slope, overturned, overarched
under the arc of sky. Crouched like soldiers,

faces hidden, whelmed at the ground.
Prisoners of other wars: tethered, tree-tied,

locked and chained: boat after boat
bound to the hard dirt bank

and left to splinter dry all winter long.
Sundown pasteling

the luminated lake, lake mirroring everything:
Water's smooth proof of boat after boat.

Shore boat / lake boat—dome / bowl—the shined flipside
of the other hand:

Because down the long inclined
far shore, beneath that wooden road

of rowboats heavy, scattered side by side, light
boat doubles float like lake's own remembrance

of their dead weight once lofted easily
like heroes on its back. More boats

oppositely upside down,
cupped, two wrongs making one right

side up against the depth of water pressed
to the sky. Below, birds flow, past trees and cloud

fish nod. And reflected in the skimming
light borrowed from a dimming sky: boat after boat after

borrowed boat—borrowed by water, by land.
Oh, boat, boat, spirit boat: I only wish that I might too

hover on the battlefield of another shore,
neither adrift nor drowned.

Variation 30: Husband

The mountains, too, are more than what they seem. Who knows with what strange yearnings they gaze down upon us: maybe they do gaze, I said, at least at you. So remember the mountains, I told her. The tender haze of their uncounted trees across the valley, their soft serrated leaves molting into brown gardens between the risers of roots you tamp in your near-silence under shelter there. Remember what you told me, how first tempting you so much you just have to climb, not for the summit but the steps, that weight when your legs stamp and lift against the heightened depths of ground, and for the webs in your way, that tint of red at the edge of newest berries, the steam off scat on stone at the blown open rim of sky, then as if with urging hands they rush you down from summits like waterfalls. Your possessive resistance either way. I said. And in stillness when you'd look up to mountains darker against dark barely lightening, and you'd wonder why this body that walks on mountains, why the trillium under ferns in May, why gangs of coyotes chaining air to the moon, why acorns raided into platters and trays on a log's riddled stump, why now, why I, why the mountains were not enough and you wanted to be taken by storm of the other world, wanted like a bride to be given away to it: I would say: Remember.

When at the planetary ridge where you would go watching again the birds you still envied that they startle gravity, fly out of bounds as if free of form, and wished you might be set loose as they are even within bones. Or without. When, I said, in the predicament of embodiment your heart by turns argues for and against the body's every dam and flood, and aches at the core for the bright crowns of fungus on trunks, the etched clawprints of bears, the night swamp of our children's hair when they stir, still asleep—still unknowing even now—remember! Because what if, I asked her, what if when you forfeit this body you still have to love everything else? I said you don't know how much less or more you may range *without* tears or touch, without the skin shifting as it did over the tendons at your neck as you curled away from me. Or how much more, while without ears you still can't help but listen the mountains then may cry out in their own unmanifest way. So please: wait. Remember. *Stay*. For the possible fall through the travail of air of a single pinecone to the ground, the blink of our children's eyes opening one last time onto a still safe world, the turn of this lover horizoned beside you on waking, hand on your scalloped spine, that intimate, helpless gaze I couldn't keep from falling toward you of the mountains at dawn.

Aria

All phases have beauty. Or in shaping time
was Bach lost to all but the count, not consonance?

One in the other, carriage and contained,
body and spirit, hitched, indivisible:

From the ground up with fractal scaffolding
he built his arc, this liquid bridge for the daily

practice of sameness, sequence, awaking
change, the brief, the sustained—and the enduring

whole bears as one all notes, as one word might
all said or sung. Where does it come from, the material

of the beautiful? And how aligned or skewed
toward discord, how reasoned with ardor and risk,

how little or much design or dumbfound—
how can we know? Grave, heavenly,

like the illumined face of a god rubbed from stone,
these breaths so wholly numbered and numinous . . .

A mere miracle of physics? Mathematics' holy writ?
Most musical web of ordered intervals framed

by symmetry, division, multiples—most melancholy
joy: Ten parallel horizons zenithed

toward always, thirty-two limiting longitudes:
A language, a form, a key. God, Johann: When in thrall

a pianist's hands arch intimate
to make the passage—to touch

your immortal body—it is as if the finite, bound,
has unwound when your *now* becomes now anew,

now mine. As if thresholds allowed recrossing: Forever
to be content, a soul at home, with a life like art

more puzzle than plan, more flight than counterweight,
the perfect grid of abiding piers upon which you

superimpose the moving force
of brilliant ephemera . . . .

Acknowledgments

Barrow Street—Essay excerpt & "Variation 9: Potter";
"Variation 14: Here after"; "Variation 19: Fish";
"Variation 23: Teatime"; "Variation 26: Winter solstice"

Chautauqua Literary Journal—"Aria"

CHEST—"Variation 27: Awakener"

Crying Sky—"Variation 12: Happy Prince's bird";
"Variation 15: Woman at the dam"; "Variation 29: Boats"

Hotel Amerika—"Variation 5: Spinning"; "Variation 21:
Dying man"

The Journal—"Variation 7: Girl"

Lyric Recovery Festival & Big City Lit Journal published
finalist—"Variation 11: Reflection"

Massachusetts Review—"Variation 18: Baker"

Mayday Magazine—"Variation 6: Snake"

National Poetry Review—"Variation 16: Actor"

No Tell Motel—"Variation 1: Yhwh"; "Variation 2: Interval";
"Variation 3: Snapping Turtle"; "Variation 4: Child";
"Variation 13: Artist"

Notre Dame Review—"Variation 3: Snapping turtle"

Slice Magazine—"Variation 22: Equivocator"

Tyger Burning—"Variation 10: Moths," "Variation 29: Boats"

Worcester Review—"Variation 24: Leatherman"

WomenArts Quarterly Journal—"Variation 25: Freed slave"

Women.Period—"Variation 7: Girl" (reprint)

Write Action Anthology—"Variation 28: Transplanted heart"

Gratitude to:

Leonard Bernstein, *The Unanswered Question* (which is Charles Ives's: "Whence music?"), videotaped Harvard Lectures series on music & language, 1973.

Erwin Bodky, *The Interpretation of Bach's Keyboard Works,* Harvard U. Press, Cambridge, 1960.

David Epstein, *Shaping Time: Music, The Brain, and Performance*, Schirmer Books, NY 1995, particularly for the opening phrase I stole: "All phases have beauty."

J.T. Fraser, *The Voices of Time* (many essays on musical analysis, rhythm & time in different cultures, arts & philosophies, etc.), Braziller, NY 1966 (OP).

Kenneth Gilbert, liner notes for *GV*, BWV988, HMC901240, 1987.

Alexandra Gorlin-Crenshaw for reading and critiquing.

Glenn Gould liner notes from his first recording of *GV*, BWV988 CBS (?) 1956.

Ralph Kirkpatrick, prefatory notes to *GV* sheet music book, Schirmer, NY 1938.

Robert L. Marshall, *The Music of Johann Sebastian Bach: The Sources, The Style, The Significance*, Schirmer Books, NY 1989.

The New Grove Dictionary of Music & Musicians, Volume One, Grove, NY 1995.

Joseph Payne, liner notes for *GV*, BWV988, Grammofon AB BIS, 1990-1991.

Timothy Alan Smith of Northern Arizona University, for various lessons on Bach, his canons, and the *GV*, at http://digitalbach.com/goldberg.

& The National Endowment for the Arts which partially supported this project.

About the Author

ALICE B. FOGEL is the poet laureate of New Hampshire and author of three previous poetry collections, most recently *Be That Empty*, a National Poetry Foundation bestseller, and the acclaimed guide to reading and appreciating poetry, *Strange Terrain: A Poetry Handbook for the Reluctant Reader*. Her poems have appeared in numerous prominent literary journals and anthologies, including The Best American Poetry series; has been nominated six times for a Pushcart Prize; and in 2012 she was the winner of the prestigious Carl Sandburg writer-in-residence award in North Carolina. She is the recipient of an Individual Artist Fellowship from the National Endowment for the Arts, among other awards. She lives in Acworth, New Hampshire.

For more information, visit her website alicebfogel.com and schaffnerpress.com

PHOTO BY MARIAH EDSON

68

Publisher's Note

THE NICHOLAS SCHAFFNER AWARD for Music in Literature celebrates the life of the publisher's brother, Nicholas Schaffner, poet, musician, esteemed music critic, and author of several books, including THE BEATLES FOREVER, THE BRITISH INVASION, and SAUCERFUL OF SECRETS: The Pink Floyd Odyssey. Nicholas, who devoted his life to music and literature about music, died in 1991 at the age of thirty-eight. This award has been created to celebrate his legacy in order to encourage those emerging writers whose lives and writing have been profoundly influenced by music. The Nicholas Schaffner Award for Music in Literature will be given to the writer of an unpublished manuscript who submits a literary work in the English language, either fiction, poetry or non-fiction (ie. memoir or essay collection) that deals in some way with the subject of music (of any genre and period) and its inspirational spirit.

For submissions guidelines for the 2016 Nicholas Schaffner Award, visit www.schaffnerpress/awards or www.schaffnerawards.com.